The Girl Who Struck Out Babe Ruth

by Jean L. S. Patrick
illustrations by Jeni Reeves

Carolrhoda Books, Inc./Minneapolis

For my grandma, Louise Schmidt, who slid into home plate
when she was 14 years old, and captured the heart
of my grandpa
— *J.L.S.P.*

The author and artist would like to thank all who provided assistance, including Lee Anderson, W. C. Burdick, Jerry Desmond, David Estabrook, Bill Francis, David Jenkins, Tom Nieman, Suzette Raney, Brad Smith, the Chattanooga-Hamilton County Bicentennial Library's Local History Department, the Chattanooga Regional History Museum, and the National Baseball Hall of Fame. And the artist would like to give special thanks to her model, Karen Dodd.

This book is available in two editions:
Library edition by Carolrhoda Books, Inc.
Soft cover by First Avenue Editions
Divisions of Lerner Publishing Group
241 First Avenue North, Minneapolis, MN 55401 U.S.A.

Website address: www.lernerbooks.com

Library of Congress Cataloging-in-Publication Data

Patrick, Jean L. S.
     The girl who struck out Babe Ruth / by Jean L. S. Patrick ; illustrated by Jeni Reeves.
          p. cm. — (On my own history)
     Summary: A retelling of the day Jackie Mitchell, a seventeen-year-old female professional baseball player, struck out the New York Yankees' best hitters, Babe Ruth and Lou Gehrig, in an exhibition game in 1931.
     ISBN 1 57505 307 7 (lib. bdg.: alk. paper)
     ISBN 1-57505-455-8 (pbk.)
     1. Mitchell, Jackie, 1914–1987—Juvenile literature. 2. Ruth, Babe, 1895–1948—Juvenile literature. 3. Gehrig, Lou, 1903–1941—Juvenile literature. [1. Mitchell, Jackie, 1914–1987. 2. Baseball players. 3. Baseball—History. 4. Women—Biography.] I. Reeves, Jeni, ill. II. Title. III. Series.
GV867.5.P377 2000
796.357'092—dc21   99-033322
     [B]

Manufactured in the United States of America
1 2 3 4 5 6 – JR – 05 04 03 02 01 00

Author's Note

Women have been playing baseball—not softball—for more than 100 years. Vassar College formed the first women's teams in 1866. Back then, a batter had to pick up her long, heavy skirt and drape it over her arm before she could run to first base.

From the 1890s through the 1930s, thousands of women played on "bloomer girl" baseball teams. Other women, such as Lizzie Murphy and Babe Didrikson, played in major league exhibition games.

One of the most talented players was Virne Beatrice "Jackie" Mitchell. When she was a young girl, baseball star Dazzy Vance taught her to pitch.

At 16, Jackie played on the Engelettes, a girls' team in Chattanooga, Tennessee. She often struck out men from semi-professional teams. A year later, in 1931, she trained with future major league players at Kid Elberfeld's famous baseball school in Atlanta.

At this time, Joe Engel was the president of the Chattanooga Lookouts, a minor league baseball team. He knew Jackie could bring great publicity to his team.

On March 25, 1931, Joe Engel announced that he would offer 17-year-old Jackie a professional contract. But Jackie couldn't sign. She was in Texas, playing in a national basketball tournament.

On Saturday, March 28, Jackie Mitchell returned to Chattanooga. Baseball was on her mind.

March 28, 1931
Chattanooga, Tennessee

Jackie Mitchell loved baseball.

She dreamed of becoming a great pitcher.

But 17-year-old Jackie

was not on the pitcher's mound.

She wasn't even at a ballpark.

She was sitting in a radio station,

wearing a dress.

In front of her was a contract.

If she signed it, she would play

for the Chattanooga Lookouts.

She would belong

to a men's minor league baseball team.

The room grew quiet.

Jackie picked up the pen.

Boldly, she signed her name.

Fans cheered.

Cameras flashed.

Mr. Joe Engel shook her hand.

He was the president of the Lookouts.

Next, Manager Bert Niehoff spoke.

He promised to help Jackie

become a pitcher in the major leagues.

Jackie and her father smiled.

But Jackie wasn't thinking

about the major leagues.

She was thinking about next week.

The Lookouts would play

the New York Yankees in a pre-season game.

On Wednesday, April 1, Jackie would face

the greatest home-run hitter in the world—

Babe Ruth.

She wanted to strike him out.

News about Jackie spread
across the country.
Big-city newspapers and film crews
planned to cover the game.
But some people wondered
about Wednesday's game.
Maybe Jackie was part of a stunt
to bring people to the ballpark.
After all, could a girl really pitch
against Babe Ruth?

She knew she could pitch
against Babe Ruth.
Even the newspapers said so.
She could put speed on the ball.
She had control.
And somehow, she could always guess
a batter's weakness.
Jackie popped a stick of gum
into her mouth.
She pretended to wind up for a pitch.
Strike!

On Tuesday night,

Jackie went to bed early.

Her uniform hung in the closet.

Ever since she was a young girl,

she had dreamed of becoming

a great pitcher.

Tomorrow was her chance

to answer that dream.

On Wednesday, rain poured from the sky.
The game was canceled.
Jackie was sure she would get to pitch
the next day.
But what if it rained again?
She'd miss her chance
to pitch against the Yankees.

On Thursday, April 2, the rain stopped.
Sunbeams, as straight as fastballs,
streamed through the clouds.
The cool air smelled of peach blossoms.
Jackie and her parents drove down
Third Street to Engel Stadium.

The Lookouts would not have an easy game.
The Yankees' new manager wanted to score
as many runs as possible.
He wanted the Yankees to win
each time they played.
Jackie and her father
watched the Yankees warm up.
Lyn Lary played shortstop.
Tony Lazzeri fielded grounders at second.
Lou Gehrig covered first base.

Babe Ruth stepped to the plate

for batting practice.

Jackie watched him closely.

He lifted his bat, twisted his body,

and swung.

Either he'd blast the ball

far into the outfield,

or he'd miss the ball completely.

Jackie wondered aloud.

How should she pitch to the Yankees?

Her father answered her.

"Go out there and pitch

just like you pitch to anyone else."

Jackie nodded.

Where could she warm up?

She spotted Eddie Kenna,

the Lookouts' catcher.

Together they trotted to an open space.

Jackie shoved her glove onto her right hand
and gripped the ball with her left.

First, the wind-up.

She wound her left arm backward
in an enormous circle.

Then, the pitch.

She side-armed the ball to the plate.

Thud.

Again and again,
the ball landed in Eddie's glove.

Jackie had a mean drop pitch.
When the ball reached home plate,
it took a nasty dip.
And when her drop pitch was working,
no batter could touch it.
But today, she struggled.
The cool, damp air
made the ball hard to control.

"Jackie!"

A man in a long coat called her name.

It was Mr. Engel.

Two towering Yankees walked beside him.

A flock of reporters followed behind.

The group stopped.

Jackie recognized Babe Ruth.

He leaned on his bat as if it were a cane.

Lou Gehrig stood at his side.

kie," said Mr. Engel.

t Mr. Ruth."

ie shook his hand.

But Babe Ruth looked away.

Then he looked at Mr. Engel.

When he finally looked at Jackie,

he dropped her hand.

"Jackie," said Mr. Engel, pointing.

"Meet Mr. Gehrig."

Lou Gehrig smiled at her.

He took off his cap.

He bowed slightly and shook her hand.

His grip was as strong as iron.

Jackie posed with the two Yankees
for photographs.
But Babe Ruth didn't smile very much.
She had heard that Babe Ruth didn't want
women playing professional baseball.
"Too delicate," he had said.
"They will never make good."
Jackie punched her glove.
She *had* to make good.

At 2:30, the stadium filled with people.
Jackie's stomach twisted.
She watched as her teammates
took the field.
Clyde Barfoot was the starting pitcher.
Eddie Kenna crouched behind home plate.
Behind him stood Brick Owens,
the famous American League umpire.
Play ball!

The Yankees batted first.

Earle Combs stepped to the plate.

He smashed the first pitch

deep into the outfield for a double.

He ran to second base.

Lyn Lary was next.
He slapped a single
into centerfield.
Earle Combs scored.
Yankees 1, Lookouts 0.

One man on.

Nobody out.

Babe Ruth was next to bat.

Eddie Kenna pulled off his mask

and trotted to the mound.

Manager Niehoff joined him.

He nodded to Jackie.

Was she ready?
Jackie grabbed her glove
and ran onto the field.
Four thousand fans cheered
from the stands.
Their noise was crushing.

Manager Niehoff wished her luck.

Eddie placed the ball in her glove.

She was in charge, he said.

She should give Babe her best.

Then he trotted back to home plate

and put on his mask.

Jackie was alone.

Her stomach twisted again.

Then she remembered her father's words.

"Go out there and pitch

just like you pitch to anyone else."

She threw a few warm-up pitches.

Her arm felt strong.

Jackie spat in her glove.

She waved Babe Ruth to the plate.

She was ready.

Babe tipped his cap.

Then he nodded to first base,

reminding her of the runner.

Jackie glanced at the runner,
then looked at Babe.
She wound up and pitched.
The ball sailed high.
"Ball one!" yelled the umpire.

Eddie tossed the ball back to her.

Jackie knew what to do.

This time she'd throw a curve ball.

This pitch would curve and drop

when it reached the plate.

Again, she glanced at the runner.

She wound up and pitched.

Babe swung.

Whoosh!

He missed.

"STRIKE ONE!" yelled the umpire.

The crowd roared.

Babe backed away from the plate.
He propped his bat against his legs
and wiped his hands.
This gave Jackie time to think.
She'd give him a fastball, shoulder high.
No one ever hit that pitch very far.
Babe stepped back to the plate.

Jackie checked the runner,

wound up, and pitched.

Babe swung.

Whoosh!

He missed again.

"STRIKE TWO!" yelled the umpire.

The crowd roared louder.

Jackie relaxed.

She was throwing the ball over the plate.

And Babe was hitting nothing but air!

She'd have to outguess him

on the next pitch.

He'd be ready for another fastball,

close and high.

But she'd fire it straight down the alley

with all the smoke she could put on it.

Babe was ready.

The crowd was silent.

Jackie checked the runner.

She wound up.

She pitched.

The pitch came in high.

Babe stopped his swing.

But the ball dropped,

cutting right over the heart of the plate.

"STRIKE THREE!" yelled the umpire.

"YOU'RE OUT!"

Babe slammed down his bat.

He hollered at the umpire.

But Jackie couldn't hear him.

Four thousand fans cheered and roared.

She had struck out the mighty Babe Ruth.

Babe stooped to pick up his bat.

He looked at Jackie.

He looked away.

Disgusted, he stomped to the dugout.

One down, thought Jackie.

Lou Gehrig stepped to the plate.

Like Babe, he was a left-handed batter.

Like Babe, he was a home-run hitter.

Jackie decided to aim for the inside
of the plate.

She'd put it a little above his waist.

Most batters had trouble with this pitch.

Jackie checked the runner on first.

She wound up and pitched.

Gehrig swung.

Whoosh!

Strike one!

Whoosh!

Strike two!

Whoosh!

Strike three!

Four thousand fans screamed
and jumped to their feet.
Jackie had faced the Yankees' best hitters.
And she had struck them out!

The Yankees went on to win, 14–4.

But the next day, Jackie's words

were in newspapers across the country.

"I am glad of having had the pleasure

of pitching against Mr. Ruth

and Mr. Gehrig," she said.

"I think they are both fine men

and great ball players.

I see nothing strange

about my striking them out,

at least stranger things have happened.

Not even the best batters can hit them all.

I only tried to do my best,

and I am the happiest girl in the world."

No longer did Jackie have to dream.

She was becoming a great pitcher.

47

Afterword

After Jackie struck out Ruth and Gehrig, she walked Tony Lazzeri. Then Manager Niehoff pulled her from the game.

But Jackie wasn't forgotten. Instead, she received fan mail from all over the country. One envelope had no address, just "The Girl Who Struck Out Babe Ruth."

Kenesaw Mountain Landis, the commissioner of baseball, also heard about the strikeouts. Landis canceled Jackie's contract with the Lookouts and banned her from professional baseball. He believed the game was too tough for women.

But Jackie continued to play baseball. From 1933 to 1937, she played with an exhibition team called the House of David. When they played the St. Louis Cardinals, she pitched against Pepper Martin, Dizzy Dean, and Leo Durocher.

Jackie died in 1987. But fans still talk about her strikeouts. Some people think that Ruth and Gehrig struck out on purpose. Maybe Joe Engel paid them to do it. After all, Engel was famous for his publicity stunts. Others think that Jackie surprised the sluggers. A drop pitch (or sinker) is hard for batters to hit, especially when they are facing a pitcher for the first time. And it wasn't unusual for Babe Ruth to strike out. During his career, he whiffed 1,330 times!

The debate will go on. But Jackie Mitchell will always be remembered as "The Girl Who Struck Out Babe Ruth."